Creative Thinking in the Classroom

Practical strategies and activities to develop innovation and critical thinking in the classroom

Published by: **Oleg Borysiuk**

Copyright © 2025 by Oleg Borysiuk

By Oleg Borysiuk

Table of Contents

By Oleg Borysiuk

Introduction

My name is Oleg, and I began my teaching career in 2017. Currently, I teach English at public schools and run my educational center in Hai Duong, Vietnam. I moved to this vibrant country in 2019, started a family, and have since fully dedicated myself to education.

Even before I began focusing on developing creative thinking in my students, I realized the importance of being creative and flexible in my own life just to manage the daily responsibilities of living and working. Being a foreigner in Vietnam has required a great deal of creativity and problem-solving skills. Navigating a new culture, language barriers, and societal norms often demands quick thinking and adaptability. Simple tasks like ordering food, communicating with locals, or finding my way around unfamiliar streets were often creative challenges. It always pushed me to think outside the box. For instance, when language failed, I relied on gestures, drawings, or even technology to communicate effectively. Adjusting to new work or social environments required flexibility and problem-solving, as I often had to find alternative ways to engage with people or tackle unexpected situations.

The classroom also threw unexpected challenges at me every day, I quickly learned that creativity wasn't just a nice-to-have. It was a necessity to stay adaptable and keep things running smoothly.

Throughout these years, I've seen firsthand the immense value of nurturing creative thinking in young minds. I've come to believe that inventiveness is not just an extra layer in education; it's a fundamental skill that empowers the young generation to navigate the complexities of the modern world. It's equips them to think critically, solve problems in new ways, and tackle whatever life throws their way.

Recognizing the need for more innovative approaches, I developed various tools and strategies to help my students unlock their creative potential. By weaving engaging activities and games into the core subjects, I aimed to create an environment where pupils felt free to explore their ideas and think outside the box. The result? A classroom is alive with curiosity, collaboration, and original thinking. I also noticed that creative games and multiple activities significantly enhanced children's understanding and mastery of core subjects, in my case English, by preventing boredom and keeping them actively engaged.

In this book, I share 10 essential aspects that I developed, refined, and mastered over time. They are designed to boost creative thinking in any class, especially when teaching English as I do. Each aspect is grounded in practical, easy-to-implement methods that can seamlessly fit into your teaching practice. I hope that educators everywhere will find these strategies helpful in unlocking their students' full creative potential and fostering a culture of innovation.

As you embark on this journey to enhance innovativeness in your classroom, remember that the goal isn't just to teach individuals how to solve problems. It's to inspire them to imagine new possibilities and take ownership of their ideas, so they can create their own paths forward.

How Creative Thinking Activities Boosted My Students' English Skills

Incorporating creative thinking activities not only sparked young minds' imagination but also significantly boosted their learning of English. By engaging in activities like open-ended discussions, brainstorming sessions, and creative problem-solving, learners naturally expanded their vocabulary, improved their critical thinking, and became more comfortable with expressing complex ideas in English. These activities encouraged them to think beyond rigid answers, leading to more fluid, confident communication.

The beauty of creative thinking is that it transcends any single subject. While it worked wonders in enhancing my students' language skills, the same principles can be applied to any subject. For instance, in Science, pupils can use creative thinking to hypothesize and explore experiments in new ways. In Math, they can develop multiple approaches to solving problems. Whether it's History, where youngsters can reimagine historical events, or Art, where creativity is at its core, the potential to enhance learning through creative thinking is limitless.

> By fostering creativity across all subjects, teachers can help pupils develop a deeper understanding of the

By Oleg Borysiuk

material, making learning more engaging, impactful, and relevant to real-world problem-solving.

What approaches and qualities teachers must possess to effectively teach creative thinking

1. Openness and Flexibility

Creative-thinking teachers should be open to new ideas and willing to adjust their teaching methods to accommodate different perspectives and learning styles. Flexibility allows room for unexpected discoveries and innovations in the classroom.

Approach: Incorporate flexible lesson plans that allow for individual input, unexpected outcomes, and unstructured creative time.

2. Encouraging Curiosity

Teachers should foster a classroom environment where curiosity is rewarded, and asking questions is a key part of the learning process. Curiosity drives creative exploration.

Approach: Ask open-ended questions, encourage inquiry-based learning, and nurture a mindset of "What if?" rather than focusing solely on correct answers.

By Oleg Borysiuk

3. Risk-taking and Experimentation

An educator who promotes creative thinking should encourage learners to take intellectual risks and try out new ideas without fear of failure. Risk-taking is essential for creativity, and mistakes should be seen as learning opportunities.

Approach: Create a classroom culture where participants feel safe to express unpolished ideas, make mistakes, and experiment with different approaches to problem-solving.

4. Modeling Creativity

Instructors must demonstrate creative thinking, showing everyone how to approach problems from multiple angles. By modeling creativity, they inspire students to do the same.

Approach: Share personal creative experiences, brainstorm ideas out loud, or solve a problem in real time to show the process of creative thinking.

5. Patience and Supportiveness

Creativity doesn't always yield immediate results, young minds need time and space to develop their ideas. Teachers must be patient and offer support throughout this process, providing constructive feedback without stifling the student's vision.

Approach: Allow enough time for reflection and revision. Offer positive reinforcement and encourage perseverance through difficult creative tasks.

6. Collaboration and Teamwork

Creative thinking often thrives in collaborative environments where diverse ideas can combine to form innovative solutions. Mentors should encourage teamwork and idea-sharing among participants.

Approach: Design group activities where pupils brainstorm or solve problems together, valuing each member's input.

7. Fostering a Growth Mindset

Teachers should cultivate a growth mindset in their pupils, helping them understand that creativity and problem-solving skills can be developed over time, rather than being innate talents.

Approach: Use language that promotes effort and growth. Remind young learners that creativity is a skill to be practiced and improved through dedication and persistence.

By Oleg Borysiuk

8. Incorporating Playfulness

Creativity often flourishes in environments that are playful and low-pressure. Teachers should incorporate games, engaging learning activities, and light-hearted challenges that spark creativity.

Approach: Introduce games that stimulate creative thinking, like "design challenges" or "improve storytelling," which encourage students to think outside the box.

9. Cross-Disciplinary Integration

Creativity is enhanced when pupils can make connections across various subjects. A teacher who integrates different disciplines (e.g., science and art, math and literature) helps youngsters see the interconnectedness of ideas.

Approach: Design projects that draw on multiple subjects and encourage young minds to explore how different fields inform one another.

10. Providing Autonomy and Choice

Giving children some control over their learning allows them to explore their interests and develop their creative voice. Teachers should provide opportunities for self-directed learning and choice-based assignments.

Approach: Offer a variety of project topics or creative tasks, letting pupils choose what resonates with them personally, thus deepening their engagement with the subject matter.

➤ By embodying these qualities and employing these approaches, educators can create a rich environment for fostering creative thinking, inventiveness, artistry, and originality, preparing young minds to face future challenges with innovation and adaptability - skills that are crucial in today's rapidly changing world.

How Creative Thinking Prepares Younger Minds for a Future Dominated by AI

Creative thinking is becoming increasingly important in a world where artificial intelligence (AI) is rapidly transforming industries. As AI takes over routine and analytical tasks, the demand for skills that machines cannot replicate (like creativity, critical thinking, and problem-solving) is growing.

Here are some statistics that illustrate why creative thinking is crucial for preparing the young generation for a future dominated by AI:

1. 65% of children entering primary school today will work in jobs that don't yet exist (World Economic Forum). Many of these future roles will require creative problem-solving and innovation, skills that AI cannot replace.

2. 85 million jobs are expected to be displaced by AI by 2025, but 97 million new roles may emerge (WEF Future of Jobs Report 2020). These new roles will demand creativity, emotional intelligence, and other human-centered abilities.

3. According to LinkedIn's 2020 Global Talent Report, creativity is the most in-demand soft skill employers seek,

followed by persuasion, collaboration, and adaptability - all enhanced through creative thinking.

4. A 2019 Adobe study found that 72% of educators believe creativity will be essential for students' success in the workforce. However, 69% also feel the current education system is not doing enough to develop these skills.

5. Creativity is projected to be among the top 3 skills required by 2025 (World Economic Forum). It's seen as a key differentiator in fields like marketing, technology, and design, where human innovation will drive growth alongside AI.

6. In a study by IBM, 60% of CEOs named "creativity" as the most critical leadership quality over the next five years, emphasizing its value in navigating the complexities of an AI-driven world.

➤ By fostering creative thinking in younger generations, educators can help students adapt to a world where AI handles routine tasks, leaving more room for human creativity, intuition, and innovation. It is obvious how important those skills are.

Now,

I think it's time to dive into the most important part of this book - the aspects of fostering creative thinking.

These aspects are not just theoretical but rooted in real-world classroom experiences. They have been developed, tested, and refined by me to help young individuals unlock their potential, think creatively, and approach challenges from fresh perspectives.

Whether you're an English teacher like myself or specialize in any other subject, these aspects are versatile and can be adapted to fit any curriculum. The key is to embrace creativity in your teaching, not as an add-on but as a fundamental part of how children learn, interact, and grow. So, let's explore these essential aspects that will enable you to foster a creative, engaged, and forward-thinking classroom environment.

10 Key Aspects for Fostering Creative Thinking in the Classroom

- ✓ **Encouraging Open-Ended Questions**
- ✓ **Providing a Safe Space for Ideas**
- ✓ **Promoting Divergent Thinking**
- ✓ **Integrating Cross-Disciplinary Learning**
- ✓ **Utilizing Creative Problem-Solving Tasks**
- ✓ **Allowing Time for Reflection**
- ✓ **Incorporating Playful Learning**
- ✓ **Encouraging Risk-Taking and Experimentation**
- ✓ **Providing Opportunities for Collaboration**
- ✓ **Modeling Creative Thinking**

These aspects helped me develop an innovative and dynamic classroom where participants feel empowered to think creatively, solve problems, and develop new ideas.

Let's dive deeper into each one of them, I'll also provide you with real, in-class examples.

Aspect 1: **Encouraging Open-Ended Questions**

Open-ended questions are one of the most effective tools for promoting creative thinking in the classroom and they are also one of my favourites. Unlike questions with a single correct answer, open-ended questions allow students to explore a variety of responses and think deeply about different possibilities. This approach not only stimulates curiosity but also helps pupils cultivate critical thinking skills as they are challenged to justify their answers and consider alternative viewpoints.

By asking questions such as "What are other ways we could solve this problem?" or "How would you improve this idea?", I encourage young learners to think beyond conventional solutions. This helps them become more confident in their thinking, as there is no "wrong" answer, just different approaches to the same problem.

Open-ended questions promote a classroom culture where exploration is valued over correctness. This shift from outcome-based learning to process-oriented thinking helps pupils feel more comfortable taking intellectual risks. As a result, they are more likely to engage in creative experimentation, which is key to innovation and problem-solving in both academic and real-world settings.

Here are 3 engaging activities that can help boost open-ended questioning skills in any classroom:

1. Think-Pair-Share with a Twist

How it works:

Present an open-ended question or problem to the class, such as "What would happen if there were no gravity?"

Give attendees time to think about their answers individually.

Then, they pair up to share their thoughts with a partner.

After discussing in pairs, students can share their responses with the entire class.

Twist: Ask pupils to challenge each other's answers with follow-up questions like, "Why do you think that would happen?" or "What evidence supports that?"

Benefit: This engaging activity cultivates deeper thinking, encourages young learners to listen carefully to their peers, and helps them practice forming thoughtful, open-ended questions in response.

By Oleg Borysiuk

Creative Response: "If there were no gravity, we would all float around like astronauts, and cities would need to be redesigned with floating platforms and tethered walkways. People might have to wear weighted suits just to stay grounded, and sports like basketball or golf would become impossible because the ball would never come down!"

Follow-up Questions:

"If we had to wear weighted suits, how might that change the way we move and interact with our surroundings in daily life? Could it spark new forms of art or entertainment?"

"Since basketball wouldn't work anymore, what kind of new sports could evolve in a gravity-free world? Could these sports actually be more fun than the ones we have now?"

These questions push young minds to think beyond the initial answer and imagine a completely different way of life.

2. Creative Scenario Building

How it works:

Divide attendees into small groups and present them with a creative, open-ended scenario (e.g., "Imagine the world runs out of electricity tomorrow. How would life change?").

Each group brainstorms multiple answers, solutions, or possibilities, and then presents their ideas to the class.

Encourage other groups to ask follow-up questions like, "What challenges would your solution face?" or "How could you expand on that idea?"

Benefit: This game encourages young learners to think outside the box, collaborate on creative solutions, and engage with one another's ideas through open-ended questioning.

Creative Responses:

If the world ran out of electricity tomorrow, life would undergo some radical transformations, but creativity and adaptability would rise to the occasion:

Back to Basics: People might return to manual tools and techniques, relying on hand-powered devices like typewriters, manual washing machines, and wood-burning stoves. Candlelit dinners would become the new norm, not for romance, but for necessity.

Community Resurgence: Local communities would grow stronger as people rely on face-to-face interactions instead of digital communication. Neighborhoods might organize barter systems or skills exchanges, like swapping fresh vegetables for carpentry work.

Creative Communication: Without the internet or phones, letter writing and creative signals like flag systems or runners might be used for long-distance communication. Town criers could return to spread important news!

Reinventing Transportation: Electric vehicles and trains would grind to a halt, but bicycles and horse-drawn carriages could see a renaissance. Solar-powered cars, pedal-powered boats, and wind-driven innovations could fill the gap.

Solar and Steam Power Boom: Renewable energy sources like solar, wind, and steam power would see a massive boost in popularity. Communities might create solar-powered cooking and lighting systems or even bring back steam engines for large-scale industries.

Urban Farming: Cities would need to transform into self-sustaining ecosystems, with rooftop gardens and public spaces converted into farmland. People would trade convenience for resilience, learning how to grow and harvest food within their own communities.

Entertainment Renaissance: Without digital distractions, live entertainment like theater, storytelling, and music would thrive again. People might start writing books by hand or learn ancient arts like shadow puppetry or outdoor cinema with pedal-powered projectors.

Innovation Surge: New ways of storing and using energy would skyrocket. Scientists and inventors would double down on exploring alternatives to electricity, possibly leading to breakthroughs in bioenergy, kinetic energy, or even rediscovering the power of natural phenomena like water currents.

In this new world, the absence of electricity would spark human creativity in unprecedented ways, forcing society to rethink how we live, work, and entertain.

Funny response:

Without electricity, we'd all become expert sun-chasers! Forget alarm clocks, we'd wake up with the sunrise and rush to get everything done before sunset - cooking, cleaning, and even trying to binge-read books by daylight. People might invent "sunlight races" where neighbors compete to finish tasks before darkness falls. And when night hits? Well, board games by candlelight would be the new Netflix binge, and you'd have to explain to your kids what a "TV" used to be!

Follow-up questions:

How would people cope with no internet memes to scroll through at night?

Could bonfires become the new social media - where people gather to "post" stories face-to-face?

3. Question Chain

How it works:

Begin by asking a broad open-ended question like, "What makes a good leader?"

The first student answers and the next must ask an open-ended question based on that response (e.g., "Can you give an example of a good leader and explain why?").

Continue around the class, with each participant building on the previous response.

Benefit: This activity builds a natural flow of discussion while helping young minds practice generating open-ended questions on the spot. It also sharpens their ability to connect ideas and engage in critical thinking.

These activities promote inquiry-based learning and stimulate curiosity, helping children become more adept at asking and answering open-ended questions.

Creative responses from one of my classes:

What makes a good leader?
A good leader listens to their team and values everyone's input.

Why is listening so important for leadership?
Listening helps leaders understand different perspectives and make informed decisions.

How do different perspectives benefit a team?
They bring creativity and innovation, solving problems more effectively.

Why is problem-solving crucial for a leader?
It helps the team overcome challenges and stay on track toward their goals.

What's one challenge leaders face when listening to everyone?
Sometimes, it's just sorting through too many ideas... especially when half the team suggests taking every Friday off!

➢ This important aspect not only supports individual creativity but also encourages collaboration, as participants can share diverse perspectives, build on each other's ideas, and engage in meaningful discussions that lead to richer learning experiences.

After a month of incorporating open-ended questions into my classroom discussions, I noticed some truly transformative effects. Pupils became more engaged and actively involved in their learning. The freedom to express their thoughts without the pressure of finding a "correct" answer encouraged them to share their ideas and opinions openly.

This shift led to a noticeable improvement in their critical thinking skills. They began analyzing and evaluating information more effectively, moving beyond simple recall to deeper comprehension. It was inspiring to witness their creativity blossom as they brainstormed innovative solutions to problems and explored various perspectives. I was even surprised by a bunch of my students' ideas!

I also saw a boost in confidence among participants who had previously been reluctant to speak up. As they practiced articulating their thoughts, they grew more assured in sharing ideas, which fostered a more inclusive classroom environment. The collaborative nature of discussions facilitated better communication, as young individuals learned to listen actively and respect differing viewpoints.

Additionally, the use of open-ended questions sparked curiosity in my students. They began asking their questions and expressing a desire to explore topics further, leading to independent research and exploration outside of class. Overall, the atmosphere in my classroom transformed into one of exploration and inquiry, empowering young minds to take ownership of their learning.

Aspect 2: **Providing a Safe Space for Ideas**

This strategy means creating an environment where attendees feel comfortable sharing their thoughts, even if those ideas are unconventional or incomplete. This approach encourages creativity, boosts confidence, and fosters an open classroom culture where all voices are heard.

Examples and ideas:

I. Classroom Discussions:

Begin with open-ended questions that have no right or wrong answers. For example, "What would happen if the sun disappeared for a week?" Students can feel free to explore wild theories without fear of judgment, knowing that their creativity is valued.

II. Group Brainstorming Sessions:

Assign group tasks where class members brainstorm solutions to a problem (e.g., "How can we reduce plastic waste in our school?"). Encourage the sharing of every idea, no matter how strange, to reinforce that all contributions are welcome. Post the ideas on a board to show that every suggestion is being considered.

III. **Mistake Celebration:**

Normalize mistakes by having pupils share something they "failed at" recently, and discuss what they learned from it. For example, "I tried to solve a math problem and got it wrong, but now I understand it better." This activity reduces the fear of failure and creates an atmosphere where learners are comfortable experimenting with new concepts.

IV. **Anonymous Idea Submission:**

Set up a "suggestion box" where everyone can anonymously submit their thoughts or ideas on class projects or school improvements. This ensures even the shyest individuals can contribute without fear of ridicule.

V. **Student-Led Projects:**

Let youngsters take the lead on projects that interest them. By giving them ownership you're showing that their ideas matter. For example, a person who loves art might design a mural for the school, while another with an interest in tech might suggest coding a class website.

Now, let's dive deeper into each one of them.

I.   Classroom Discussions

A real example of this could be a discussion around a historical event, like the Industrial Revolution. Instead of asking students to simply recount facts, ask an open-ended question like, "How do you think our world would be different today if the Industrial Revolution never happened?"

This question doesn't have a right or wrong answer and allows young minds to explore creative, divergent thinking. One person might suggest that we'd all still be living in rural communities, while another might propose that technology would have developed in different, unexpected ways. By encouraging a range of responses, you're allowing participants to feel safe sharing ideas without fear of being "wrong."

Follow up by asking them to expand on their ideas, such as "What are some specific technologies or industries that would have never developed?" or "How would daily life look different without the Industrial Revolution?" This opens the floor for deeper thought and broader participation.

Here are some model answers for the open-ended question on the Industrial Revolution from one of my classes:

Question: How do you think our world would be different today if the Industrial Revolution never happened?

Student 1: *"If the Industrial Revolution never happened, I think most people would still live in rural areas and work on farms. Cities wouldn't have grown as quickly because factories were a big reason people moved to urban areas. We'd still rely on handmade goods, and technology like trains and cars might have taken much longer to develop."*

Student 2: *"Without the Industrial Revolution, the world might be less polluted. Since factories and machines are big contributors to air pollution, maybe our environment would be healthier today. People would have kept using simpler technologies, like windmills or nature-powered machinery, which would have been better for the environment."*

Student 3: *"I think technology would have taken a different path. Instead of steam power, we might have relied more on renewable energy sources earlier on, like wind or water. Maybe we'd have advanced in solar power much sooner and faster because we wouldn't have focused so much on coal and steam."*

Student 4: *"Our daily lives would be really different. We wouldn't have all the mass-produced items we use today, everything would be made by hand. Things like clothes, furniture, and even books would be much more expensive and harder to get because they would take longer to produce."*

Student 5: *"Transportation would be slower. Without trains and steamships, we might still be using horses and carriages to get around. It would take much longer to travel, and global trade would have been limited because shipping goods across oceans would have been slower and more expensive."*

Follow-up questions and model answers:

What are some specific technologies or industries that would have never developed? *"Steam engines, factories, and mass production lines wouldn't exist. This would have delayed the invention of cars, planes, and maybe even electricity-based inventions like the light bulb or telephone."*

How would daily life look different without the Industrial Revolution? *"We'd still be using handmade goods, and life would move at a slower pace. People would spend more time growing their own food or making clothes. Technology would be much more basic - there'd be no mass-produced items like we have today."*

By Oleg Borysiuk

These model answers give pupils the freedom to express their thoughts while demonstrating critical thinking and creativity.

II.   Group Brainstorming Sessions

Assign group tasks where learners brainstorm solutions to a problem (e.g., "How can we reduce plastic waste in our school?"). Encourage the sharing of every idea, no matter how strange, to reinforce that all contributions are welcome. Post the ideas on a board to show that every suggestion is being considered.

Real Example of a Group Brainstorming Session:

Facilitator (Teacher): *"Alright, class, let's brainstorm ways we can reduce plastic waste in our school. Remember, every idea is welcome, even the wild ones!"*

Student 1: *"We could ban plastic water bottles and have everyone use reusable ones instead. The school could even give out reusable bottles with the school logo!"*

Student 2: *"How about setting up more recycling bins around the school? Maybe we could have one in every classroom and in the hallways, so it's easier to recycle."*

Student 3: *"What if the cafeteria stopped using plastic utensils and containers? They could switch to biodegradable ones or even encourage students to bring their own forks and spoons."*

Student 4: *"I think we should start a 'Plastic-Free Day' once a week where everyone brings lunch in reusable containers, and there's no plastic allowed anywhere in the school for the whole day!"*

Student 5: *"We could organize a competition where each class tries to reduce the most plastic waste. The winning class gets a reward, like a pizza party or an extra recess!"*

Student 6: *"We could work with local stores to encourage them to give students a discount if they bring their own bags instead of using plastic ones when they go shopping."*

Student 7: *"Maybe we can do a fundraiser to buy refill stations for water bottles. That way, students don't have to buy plastic bottles when they forget their reusable ones."*

Model Answers for Follow-Up Discussion:

Teacher: *"What are some specific actions we can take to reduce plastic in the cafeteria?"*

Student 1: *"We could talk to the cafeteria staff about switching to paper straws and using reusable trays instead of plastic containers."*

By Oleg Borysiuk

Teacher: *"How can we encourage more students to recycle in school?"*

Student 2: *"We could make posters that show what items go in each recycling bin, and maybe even have a class project where we teach other students how to recycle properly."*

Teacher: *"What incentives would get students more involved in reducing plastic waste?"*

Student 3: *"Rewards like a pizza party for the class that reduces the most plastic, or points for eco-friendly actions that add up to fun prizes, like reusable lunch bags."*

Teacher: *"How can we involve the community outside of school to help with this effort?"*

Student 4: *"We could invite local businesses to join us in reducing plastic. Maybe they could offer discounts to students who bring reusable containers or bags."*

Final Ideas from the Session:

- Ban plastic water bottles in school and offer reusable alternatives.
- Increase recycling bins across the campus with clear labels.
- Switch to biodegradable utensils and containers in the cafeteria.
- Implement a Plastic-Free Day once a week.

- Organize a class competition to reduce plastic waste.
- Work with local stores to encourage discounts for using reusable bags.
- Fundraise for water bottle refill stations around the school.

These examples reflect creative and actionable ideas, helping pupils think practically and collaboratively about reducing plastic waste. By engaging in these discussions and activities, young learners not only develop critical thinking and problem-solving skills but also foster a sense of responsibility toward their environment. This collaborative approach encourages them to see the impact of their actions, promoting a mindset focused on sustainability and community well-being.

Ultimately, these efforts contribute to growing a better society - one that values innovation and collective action to tackle pressing global issues like plastic waste. Through their involvement, the young generation learns that they can be change-makers, inspiring others to adopt similar practices and advocate for a healthier planet.

III.   Mistake Celebration:

Normalize mistakes by having students share something they "failed" at recently, and discuss what they learned from it. For example, "I tried to solve a math problem and got it wrong,

By Oleg Borysiuk

but now I understand it better." This activity reduces the fear of failure and creates an atmosphere where children are comfortable experimenting with new concepts.

Mistake Celebration Session:

Scenario: A pupil tried to solve a math problem and got it wrong, but now understands the concept better.

Example of a Mistake Celebration Session

Teacher (Facilitator): *"Today, we're going to celebrate mistakes! Mistakes are how we learn and grow, so let's give a round of applause for anyone brave enough to share one! Who would like to go first?"*

Student 1: *"I tried to solve a math problem in our last homework, but I got it wrong. I thought I understood it, but when I checked the answer, I realized I had confused the steps. After going over it again, I finally got how to solve it."*

Teacher: *"Great! Let's dig into this. What was the math problem, and what part of it did you find confusing?"*

Student 1: *"It was about solving for X in an equation, and I messed up when I was isolating the variable. I forgot to divide both sides by the coefficient of X."*

Teacher: *"That's a really common mistake! Can you explain how you approached it after you realized your error?"*

Student 1: *"Yeah, once I understood that part, I went back and remembered to divide both sides by the coefficient, which made the rest of the problem much clearer."*

Teacher: *"Awesome! Now you've got it. What do you think you learned from making that mistake?"*

Student 1: *"I learned to slow down and check each step, instead of just rushing to get to the answer."*

Teacher (to the class): *"See, this is a great example of how mistakes can teach us! Sometimes we're in such a hurry to finish the problem that we skip important steps. Now that you've made this mistake and learned from it, you're less likely to make it again. Does anyone else want to share a mistake they've learned from?"*

Model Answers for Follow-Up Discussion:

Teacher: *"Why do you think it's important to make mistakes when learning something new?"*

Student 2: *"Because mistakes show us what we don't understand yet, and that helps us focus on what we need to work on."*

Teacher: *"How can making mistakes help us understand concepts better?"*

By Oleg Borysiuk

Student 3: *"When we get something wrong and figure out why, we remember it better next time. It sticks in our minds more than just getting it right the first time."*

Teacher: *"What can you do when you're feeling frustrated after making a mistake?"*

Student 4: *"Take a break, go back to it later, and try to understand where I went wrong instead of just giving up."*

Teacher: *"Has anyone ever made a mistake that led to a breakthrough in understanding? How did that feel?"*

Student 5: *"I felt really good! I was upset when I got the problem wrong at first, but then when I finally understood it, I was proud of myself for figuring it out."*

Key Ideas to Reinforce:

Mistakes are learning opportunities.

It's not about getting the right answer but understanding the process.

Everyone makes mistakes, and they can lead to deeper learning and growth.

The goal of a Mistake Celebration session is to normalize mistakes, promote growth mindsets, and encourage young minds to learn from their errors without fear of judgment.

IV.   Anonymous Idea Submission:

Set up a "suggestion box" where attendees can anonymously submit their thoughts or ideas on class projects or school improvements. This ensures even the shyest person can contribute without fear of ridicule.

Anonymous Idea Submission Session Example

Objective: To encourage participants to share ideas freely without fear of judgment or criticism by submitting them anonymously.

Scenario:

The class is working on improving the school environment, and the teacher sets up an anonymous idea submission session for ways to make the school more eco-friendly.

Session Plan:

Teacher's Introduction: *"Today, we're going to brainstorm ideas on how we can make our school more eco-friendly. But this time, we're doing things a little differently. Instead of raising hands or sharing out loud, I want each of you to write down your ideas anonymously. You won't have to worry about whether your idea is perfect - this is all about creativity! Once you've written it down, place it in the box here at the front."*

(The teacher hands out small slips of paper or allows students to submit digitally via an anonymous online platform, depending on the classroom setup.)

Student Idea Submission: *Students take 5-10 minutes to think and write their suggestions. Since the ideas are anonymous, students may feel more comfortable submitting ideas they wouldn't normally share.*

Collecting Ideas: *After all ideas are submitted, the teacher mixes them up and reads them aloud to the class.*

Teacher Reads the First Idea: *"Our first idea is: 'We could install more recycling bins around the school and label them clearly for different materials like paper, plastic, and aluminum.'"*

Teacher's Response: *"That's a really practical suggestion! We could definitely reduce waste if everyone recycled properly. How many of you think that more labeled bins could make a big difference?"*

Teacher Reads the Second Idea: *"Here's another one: 'We should start a school garden where students can grow their own vegetables and flowers, and learn about sustainability.'"*

Teacher's Response: *"What a creative idea! A school garden could be a great way to get hands-on experience with nature and sustainability. Plus, we could use the vegetables in the canteen. How many of you would be interested in helping with something like that?"*

Teacher Reads the Third Idea: *"This one says: 'We could hold a competition to see which class can use the least amount of paper for a week. The winning class gets a reward!"*

Teacher's Response: *"I love the competitive spirit behind this idea! It's a fun way to get everyone involved in reducing waste. What kind of reward do you think would be motivating for the winning class?"*

Discussion and Follow-Up: *The teacher opens up the floor for further discussion on the ideas, encouraging the class to vote on which ideas they'd like to pursue. Since the suggestions were anonymous, students felt more comfortable discussing them openly.*

By Oleg Borysiuk

Key Benefits of Anonymous Idea Submission:

✓ *No Fear of Judgment:* Pupils are more likely to share unique or unconventional ideas without the worry of being judged or embarrassed.

✓ *Encourages Participation:* Even quieter individuals who are reluctant to speak up feel empowered to contribute.

✓ *Diverse Ideas:* The anonymity leads to a wider range of creative ideas since students aren't afraid of standing out or being different.

Follow-Up Activity:

After the session, the teacher could choose to implement one or two of the ideas with the help of the learners. This creates a sense of ownership and involvement for everyone.

This session fosters a collaborative environment where young voices are heard equally, helping build confidence and creativity in problem-solving.

V.   Student-Led Projects

Let attendees take the lead on projects that interest them. By giving them ownership, you're showing that their ideas matter. For example, a person who loves art might design a mural for the school, while another with an interest in tech might suggest coding a class website.

Student-Led Projects Session Example

Objective: To encourage young minds to take ownership of their learning by planning and executing a project of their choice related to a curriculum topic, with minimal teacher intervention.

Scenario:

The class is studying environmental science, focusing on sustainability. The instructor wants class members to choose a specific sustainability issue to research and create a project around it. Each group will lead their own project from start to finish, while the teacher provides guidance when needed.

Session Plan:

Teacher's Introduction:

"We've been learning about sustainability, but now it's time for you to take the lead! Each of you will work in groups to choose a sustainability topic that interests you and develop a project around it. This can be a research project, a community initiative, or a creative presentation - whatever you think will make an impact. You'll be in charge of every aspect: planning, organizing, and executing. My role is just to guide you if you need help."

Group Formation:

The class is divided into small groups, each consisting of 3-5 pupils. They are encouraged to pick members they feel they can collaborate well with.

Project Brainstorming:

Each group spends 15-20 minutes discussing potential project ideas. The teacher provides a framework of questions to guide the brainstorming:

"What sustainability issue are you most passionate about?"

"How can your project make a positive impact on this issue?"

"Who will benefit from your project?"

Example of Group Discussions:

Group 1:

"I think we should focus on reducing plastic waste in our school."

"Maybe we can design posters and campaigns to raise awareness about how to recycle better."

Group 2:

"What if we create a school garden and teach students how to grow vegetables sustainably?"

"We could use the produce in the cafeteria. That would be cool!"

Teacher Check-In:

After the brainstorming phase, the teacher checks in with each group briefly to ensure they have a clear direction. This is where the teacher offers guidance if groups are struggling.

Teacher's Support:

"I love the idea of a school garden! Have you thought about where you could set it up and what supplies you'll need?"

By Oleg Borysiuk

"If you want to start a recycling campaign, you'll need to think about how to promote it effectively. Maybe you could use social media or make announcements at school assemblies?"

Project Planning:

Each group creates a timeline for their project, outlining key tasks and deadlines. They assign roles within the group, such as project leader, researcher, and presenter.

Example Plan for Group 1 (Plastic Waste Reduction Project):

Week 1: Research and gather information on plastic waste.

Week 2: Design posters and educational materials.

Week 3: Present the campaign to the school and hang posters.

Week 4: Track recycling efforts and evaluate the project's success.

Project Execution:

Over the course of several weeks, each group works on their project independently. They may need to collaborate with other departments or reach out to the community, depending on the nature of their project.

Final Presentation:

At the end of the project timeline, each group presents their findings or results to the class. This can be in the form of a PowerPoint presentation, a video, a live demonstration, or a creative display.

Example Presentation (Group 1):

Group 1 presents data on plastic waste reduction efforts at the school, showing how their awareness campaign led to a 20% increase in recycling over the month.

Teacher's Feedback:

After each presentation, the mentor aims to provide a constructive feedback, focusing on both the strengths and areas for improvement. The teacher also encourages peer feedback, allowing pupils to reflect on their classmates' work.

Teacher's Feedback Example:

"Group 1, your plastic waste reduction campaign was incredibly well-organized. I can see the impact it had on the school! For your next project, think about how you could expand it further, maybe by collaborating with local businesses."

Benefits of Student-Led Projects:

✓ *Empowerment:* Participants take full ownership of their learning, develop leadership and project management skills.

✓ *Collaboration:* Young individuals learn how to work effectively in groups, delegating tasks and managing time.

✓ *Problem-Solving:* Each group tackles a real-world issue, helping them apply their knowledge in practical ways.

✓ *Creativity:* Students are encouraged to think outside the box and come up with innovative solutions.

Follow-Up Activity:

After the presentations, the class can vote on which projects should be implemented or expanded, with the winning group having the opportunity to take their project to a larger scale, such as a school-wide or community initiative.

This Student-Led Session not only engages learners but also fosters responsibility, teamwork, and critical thinking while allowing participants to explore topics they care about in the most meaningful way.

➢ Creating a Safe Space for Ideas allows pupils to develop critical thinking and problem-solving skills while building confidence in their unique abilities.

Aspect 3: **Promoting Divergent Thinking**

Promoting Divergent Thinking is about encouraging the young generation to think creatively and explore multiple solutions to a problem rather than sticking to a single, linear answer. Divergent thinking fosters innovation and helps learners develop the ability to generate a variety of ideas, solutions, or approaches. By promoting this skill, educators can help students build critical thinking and problem-solving capabilities, which are essential for success in a complex world.

Example Session: "How Can We Improve Our School's Outdoor Spaces?"

Objective: To encourage pupils to think divergently by exploring multiple creative solutions to enhance their school's outdoor areas.

1. Introduction:

The teacher introduces the session by explaining the concept of divergent thinking: *"Today, we're going to think in a way that has no wrong answers! Divergent thinking is all about coming up with as many ideas as we can. Remember, even the craziest ideas can lead to the best solutions."*

2. The Problem:

The instructor presents a real-world problem for attendees to solve: *"Our school's outdoor spaces need improvement. What are some ways we could make them more inviting, useful, or fun for students?"*

3. Brainstorming (Divergent Phase):

Students are encouraged to share all ideas, no matter how wild or unconventional they are. The teacher writes every idea on the board without evaluating or criticizing any suggestions.

Example Ideas:

"We could plant a school garden where students grow vegetables and flowers!"

"How about building an outdoor classroom so we can have lessons outside?"

By Oleg Borysiuk

"We could set up a recycling station or art installations made from recyclable materials!"

"Let's create a space with benches and shade where students can relax during breaks."

"How about putting up a mural wall where students can paint and express themselves creatively?"

"We could add a playground with swings and climbing equipment!"

4. Grouping Ideas (Convergent Phase):

Once the brainstorming is complete, the mentor helps youngsters categorize ideas into themes or groups:

Sustainability (e.g., school garden, recycling station)

Learning Spaces (e.g., outdoor classroom, mural wall)

Recreational Spaces (e.g., playground, relaxation area)

5. Voting and Selection:

Pupils vote on the ideas they are most excited about, and the class selects a few top ideas to explore further.

6. Planning the Next Steps:

The teacher guides class members in thinking about the next steps to implement the chosen ideas. They work in groups to develop action plans for how the selected projects could be realized.

7. Reflection:

The educator wraps up the session by discussing how divergent thinking allowed them to explore many possibilities: *"Look how many creative ideas we came up with today! It's important to remember that there isn't just one solution to a problem. By thinking differently, we can come up with ideas that are unique and inspiring."*

Benefits of Divergent Thinking activities:

✓ *Encourages Creativity:* Students learn to think outside the box and approach problems from different angles.

✓ *Builds Confidence:* When learners see that their ideas are valued, they become more confident in sharing thoughts and solutions.

✓ *Enhances Collaboration:* Brainstorming and idea-sharing promote teamwork and collective problem-solving.

✓ *Develops Critical Thinking:* Young minds practice evaluating and organizing a wide range of ideas, learning to identify the best solutions.

➢ By incorporating sessions like these into the classroom, instructors can foster an environment where creativity flourishes and learners are empowered to think innovatively.

Aspect 4: **Integrating Cross-Disciplinary Learning**

Integrating Cross-Disciplinary Learning involves combining different subjects or disciplines to create a holistic learning experience. This approach encourages pupils to draw connections between various areas of knowledge, enhancing their understanding of how different subjects interact in real-world scenarios.

Example Session: "Designing a Sustainable City" (Combining Geography, Science, and Math)

Objective: Attendees will apply concepts from geography, environmental science, and mathematics to design a sustainable city. This will allow them to explore urban planning, sustainability, and resource management while integrating knowledge from multiple subjects.

1. Introduction:

The instructor begins by explaining the challenge: *"Today, we're going to design a sustainable city. To do this, we'll need to think like geographers, scientists, and mathematicians. Our goal is to create a city that could balance human needs with environmental sustainability."*

2. Geography Component (Understanding the Land):

Students learn about different types of landforms and climates and how they affect city planning.

The teacher asks: *"What factors should we consider when choosing where to build our city? How does the environment—such as the location of rivers, mountains, and forests—impact how we design cities?"*

Class members research and select a location for their city based on geographical features (e.g., near a river for water supply or in a temperate climate for easier living conditions).

3. Environmental Science Component (Sustainability):

The focus shifts to environmental sustainability, with attendees discussing renewable energy, waste management, and green spaces.

The mentor explains concepts like solar and wind energy, and recycling systems, then asks: *"How can we ensure our city uses resources sustainably? What renewable energy sources should we use, and how will we manage waste and pollution?"*

Pupils incorporate solar panels, wind turbines, and recycling centers into their city designs.

4. Math Component (Urban Planning and Resource Allocation):

In this stage, young learners use mathematical concepts to design the layout of their city. They calculate the area for different zones (residential, commercial, industrial) and decide how resources (e.g., energy, water) will be distributed.

The teacher asks: *"How much space will we need for housing, schools, and parks? How can we calculate the amount of energy and water needed for the city's population?"*

Students use basic geometry to sketch a layout and perform calculations to determine energy needs, the size of green spaces, and the number of buildings required.

5. Group Collaboration and Presentation:

In groups, learners work together to design their city, combining geographical considerations, environmental practices, and mathematical calculations.

They then present their cities to the class, explaining their choices: *"Our city is located near a river for fresh water and transport. We've installed solar panels on every building and included lots of parks to improve air quality. We calculated that we'd need 100 wind turbines to power the entire city."*

6. Reflection and Discussion:

The teacher wraps up the session by leading a reflection on how each discipline contributed to the project: *"How did geography, science, and math help you create your city? What challenges did you face in balancing human needs with environmental sustainability?"*

Benefits of Cross-Disciplinary Learning:

✓ *Real-World Application:* Pupils see how different subjects work together to solve complex problems.

✓ *Collaborative Skills:* Working in groups fosters communication and teamwork, as students combine their strengths across disciplines.

✓ *Critical Thinking:* Young minds develop their problem-solving skills by considering multiple perspectives and constraints.

> ➤ In this session, youngsters not only learned about sustainability and urban planning, but they also saw how geographical knowledge, scientific principles, and math skills are interconnected in real-world situations. This helps them recognize the value of learning across different subjects.

Aspect 5: **Utilizing Creative Problem-Solving Tasks**

Utilizing Creative Problem-Solving Tasks encourages juniors to think critically, generate unique solutions, and approach challenges from multiple perspectives. These tasks can stimulate innovation and foster a growth mindset in the classroom.

Real Example Session: "Rescue the Stranded Astronaut" (STEM-focused Creative Problem-Solving)

Objective: Students will use creativity, engineering principles, and teamwork to design a method to rescue a stranded astronaut on Mars, applying critical thinking and problem-solving skills.

1. Introduction:

The instructor introduces the challenge: *"Imagine an astronaut is stranded on Mars, and your mission is to rescue them. You'll need to use the resources available on Mars and your engineering skills to create a rescue plan. How can you get them back to safety?"*

Pupils are given limited "resources" (e.g., cardboard, string, rubber bands, straws, and tape) to work with, simulating the constraints astronauts would face on Mars.

2. Problem Definition:

Children discuss the problem in groups and brainstorm potential challenges: *"What are the main obstacles we need to overcome? What's the most important part of our mission?"*

Ideas such as the lack of oxygen, the harsh Martian environment, and the need for a sturdy vehicle are discussed. The teacher guides them to break the problem down into smaller, more manageable tasks (e.g., how to build a safe vehicle or device with the given materials).

3. Brainstorming Solutions:

Learners are encouraged to come up with multiple solutions, no matter how unconventional: *"What are some ways we can transport the astronaut safely across Mars? Could we build a vehicle? A shelter? How could we use gravity or wind?"*

They are given time to sketch their ideas on paper before choosing one solution to develop.

4. Prototyping and Testing:

Students use the provided materials to build a prototype based on their chosen solution. During this phase, creativity and experimentation are key: *"What's the best way to construct the vehicle with limited resources? Can we test how it moves or protects the astronaut from harsh conditions?"*

The teacher encourages trial and error, prompting students to test their ideas and refine them: *"Does your design work as expected? What could you change to make it better?"*

If a solution doesn't work, participants are encouraged to go back to the drawing board and revise their approach.

5. Presentation of Solutions:

Each group presents their design to the class, explaining how it would work to rescue the astronaut: *"We designed a rover using cardboard and rubber bands to absorb impact. It has an oxygen tank made of straws and is covered in a protective layer to shield the astronaut from dust storms."*

They explain the challenges they faced and how they overcame them, demonstrating their creative thinking process.

6. Reflection and Discussion:

The session concludes with a class discussion about the creative problem-solving process: *"What was the hardest part of the task? How did creativity help you come up with your solution? What would you do differently next time?"*

The teacher emphasizes the importance of thinking outside the box and not being afraid to fail: *"Did you learn more from the designs that didn't work? How did your team's creativity lead to innovative solutions?"*

Benefits of Creative Problem-Solving Tasks:

✓ *Encourages Critical Thinking:* Students must analyze problems and consider different angles and solutions.

✓ *Fosters Innovation:* Open-ended tasks allow for unique, unexpected ideas, pushing young minds to think beyond conventional approaches.

✓ *Builds Resilience:* Pupils learn that failure is part of the process, helping them develop a growth mindset and persistence.

➢ In this session, class members were tasked with solving a real-world challenge in a simulated context, requiring them to use their creativity and problem-solving skills. The open-ended nature of the task encouraged them to explore various ideas and build a functional prototype under real constraints, just like real engineers or scientists would.

Aspect 6: **Allowing Time for Reflection**

Allowing Time for Reflection is an essential part of learning. It encourages pupils to think critically about their learning process, assess their understanding, and connect new knowledge with prior experiences. Reflection fosters deeper insights, self-awareness, and personal growth, giving students the opportunity to internalize their learning.

Real Example Session: "What Did I Learn Today?"

Objective: At the end of a lesson or project, attendees reflect on what they've learned, how they approached problems, and how they can improve in the future.

1. Introduction:

After completing a group project on environmental sustainability, the instructor allocates the last 10-15 minutes of the class for individual reflection: *"Before we end today, let's take some time to reflect on what we've learned and how we worked together."*

2. Reflective Prompts:

The teacher gives each student a set of guiding questions to help them organize their thoughts: *"What new concepts or skills did I learn today? What did I do well? What could I have done differently to improve my learning or teamwork?"*

Learners can write down their thoughts or record their reflections verbally in pairs.

3. Group Sharing:

After individual reflection, pupils are asked to share one key takeaway with their peers in small groups: *"Share one thing you're proud of from today's work and one thing you'd like to improve on next time."*

This encourages participants to articulate their insights and learn from others' experiences.

4. Teacher-Led Reflection Discussion:

The educator then leads a whole-class reflection, guiding students through deeper questions: *"How did your group solve problems together? What was challenging? How did you overcome these challenges? How will today's lesson change how you approach future projects?"*

By Oleg Borysiuk

This helps pupils connect their learning to real-world applications, and recognize areas where they can improve or change their approach.

5. Reflection Journals:

As a follow-up, youngsters are asked to maintain reflection journals where they can regularly document their thoughts and growth: *"Continue writing in your journal at the end of each project. Think about how you've grown since the beginning of the semester."*

The teacher reviews these journals periodically to offer personalized feedback, helping students track their own progress over time.

6. Closing the Session:

The mentor emphasizes the importance of reflection in personal growth: *"Reflection helps you see how far you've come and where you still want to go. It's not just about the final result, but the journey of learning and improving."*

The session ends with class participants feeling more mindful of their learning process and ready to take these insights into their next projects.

Benefits of Reflection:

✓ *Encourages Self-Assessment:* Students learn to evaluate their own strengths and areas for improvement.

✓ *Fosters Metacognition:* It promotes thinking about thinking, which helps individuals become aware of their learning strategies.

✓ *Boosts Confidence:* Reflection allows learners to recognize their accomplishments, reinforcing a sense of achievement.

✓ *Promotes Continuous Learning:* By identifying areas for improvement, young minds are more likely to seek out new knowledge and strategies.

✓ *Supports Emotional Growth:* Reflecting on various challenges and successes helps juniors develop resilience and emotional intelligence.

➢ In this session, students had time to step back and think about their learning journey. By providing space for reflection, the instructor enabled them to internalize their growth, identify personal strengths, and set goals for future learning experiences. This process transforms learning from a one-time event into a continuous, self-driven practice.

Aspect 7: **Incorporating Playful Learning**

Incorporating playful learning into the classroom can make lessons more engaging, foster creativity, and deepen learners' understanding of key concepts. Here are 10 examples of games and activities that promote playful learning across different subjects:

1. Learning Through Role-Play

Example: *History Role-Play* - Students act out historical events, such as a debate between historical figures. This helps them understand the context of decisions made in history and develop empathy for different perspectives.

2. Math Scavenger Hunt

Example: *Find the Math in Your World* - Create a scavenger hunt where participants must find objects that match given mathematical properties (e.g., find something that has the shape of a triangle or a number divisible by 5). This makes math interactive and relevant to real-world applications.

3. Science Pictionary

Example: *Draw That Concept* - In groups, students take turns drawing science concepts (like photosynthesis, gravity, or chemical reactions) on the board while their teammates guess. This reinforces visual learning and understanding of scientific processes.

4. Vocabulary Bingo

Example: *Bingo With a Twistb* - Each square on the bingo card has a vocabulary word, and the teacher gives the definition or uses the word in a sentence. Learners must mark the correct word, reinforcing vocabulary acquisition in a fun way.

5. Story Cubes

Example: *Creative Writing Dice* - Students roll dice that have pictures or symbols on them and use the images to create a story. This encourages creativity and helps young minds with story structure and imaginative thinking.

6. Puzzle-Based Problem Solving

Example: *Escape Room Math* - Set up an escape room scenario where attendees must solve math problems or answer questions to unlock clues and "escape" the classroom. This boosts problem-solving skills and teamwork in a fun, competitive environment.

7. Hot Seat Debate

Example: *Debate Game* - One person sits in the "hot seat" and takes on a character or position on a controversial issue. The class asks them questions, and the student has to defend his/her stance. This significantly improves critical thinking, communication skills, and also understanding of diverse perspectives.

8. Word Wall Battles

Example: *Grammar Wall Game* - Divide participants into teams and create a wall of vocabulary or grammar rules. Teams compete to use as many words or rules as possible in correct sentences within a time limit. This fosters fast thinking and reinforces language skills.

9. Geography Around the World

Example: *Global Explorer Race* - Each group receives a country they "visit" by answering geography-related questions (e.g., capital cities, flags, landmarks). Students race to different stations around the room, adding an element of movement and competition to geography learning.

10. Art Through Music

Example: *Paint What You Hear* - Play different types of music and ask learners to paint or draw what they visualize. This integrates art and music, encouraging creativity and emotional expression while allowing individuals to interpret abstract concepts.

➤ These activities and games bring playful learning into the classroom, helping students engage with the material in fun and innovative ways. They also promote collaboration, critical thinking, and creativity, which are essential skills for lifelong learning.

Aspect 8: **Encouraging Risk-Taking and Experimentation**

Encouraging Risk-Taking and Experimentation in the classroom fosters a growth mindset where students feel safe to explore, make mistakes, and try unconventional approaches without fear of failure. This approach builds confidence and resilience, essential skills for both academic success and personal growth.

By creating a space where mistakes are seen as learning opportunities, pupils are more likely to push beyond their comfort zones and experiment with new ideas. Instructors can model this by praising effort, curiosity, and creative problem-solving, rather than focusing on correct answers.

For instance, in a STEM challenge like building the tallest tower with limited materials (e.g., spaghetti and marshmallows), youngsters are encouraged to take risks with different designs, knowing that failure is part of the process. Through this, they learn to adapt, iterate, and develop innovative solutions, ultimately building confidence in their ability to tackle complex problems.

Real Example of a Session: Encouraging Risk-Taking and Experimentation

Objective:

Encourage class members to step out of their comfort zones, take risks, and embrace failure as part of the learning process, particularly in a STEM (Science, Technology, Engineering, Math) context.

Topic: "Building the Tallest Tower" (STEM Challenge)

Session Overview:

Grade Level: Middle School

Subject: STEM (can also be adapted to other subjects)

Duration: 60 minutes

Materials Needed:

Marshmallows

Spaghetti (uncooked)

Tape

String

Measuring tape

Timer (optional)

Step-by-Step Breakdown:

Introduction to the Challenge (10 minutes):

Begin by explaining the activity: Students will work in teams to build the tallest free-standing tower they can using only marshmallows and uncooked spaghetti. The goal is to see who can build the tallest structure that remains standing after 5 minutes.

Encourage them to think creatively and experiment with different designs. Let them know that failure is part of the process and that learning comes from testing ideas, even if they don't work out.

Setting the Ground Rules (5 minutes):

Pupils are only allowed to use the materials provided (spaghetti, marshmallows, string, and tape).

They will have 20 minutes to build their towers.

Towers must be free-standing (i.e., cannot be supported by desks, chairs, or any other external structures).

Remind participants that there are no penalties for failed attempts. The focus is on experimentation, risk-taking, and learning from mistakes.

Building Time (20 minutes):

Teams get to work on constructing their towers.

Encourage them to try out different approaches. Some may want to build a strong base, while others may focus on height first.

During this time, circulate around the classroom and ask questions like:

"What are you trying to achieve with that design?"

"What happens if you try it this way?"

"How could you make your structure stronger?"

When students' towers fall, celebrate their effort, and ask what they learned from the attempt.

Evaluation and Reflection (15 minutes):

Once time is up, measure the towers and see which ones can stand on their own for at least 5 minutes.

After the challenge, gather all members for a reflection session. Ask questions such as:

"What challenges did you face during the activity?"

"Did you change your approach after something didn't work? If so, how?"

"What did you learn from the experience of failing and trying again?"

"How did taking risks with your design lead to success or failure?"

Highlight that the process of trial and error is an important part of innovation and problem-solving.

Celebrating Risk-Taking (10 minutes):

Acknowledge individuals who took creative or unconventional approaches, even if their towers didn't succeed. Reward risk-takers by sharing their insights with the class and discussing how they adapted to challenges.

Emphasize that risk-taking and experimentation are valuable skills not just in STEM but in all aspects of life.

Outcome and Reflection:

Youngsters learned that failure is part of the process of innovation. Many teams had towers collapse multiple times but continued experimenting with different designs.

By the end of the session, some pupils built successful towers, while others gained a deeper understanding of what didn't work and why.

A key takeaway was that stepping out of one's comfort zone and testing new ideas, even with the possibility of failure, is a vital part of learning and growth.

➢ This session illustrates the importance of encouraging risk-taking in a safe, supportive environment. By framing failure as a natural part of the learning process, learners can feel empowered to explore new ideas without fear of negative consequences.

By Oleg Borysiuk

Aspect 9: **Providing Opportunities for Collaboration**

Providing Opportunities for Collaboration is key to developing teamwork, communication, and critical thinking skills in young individuals. Collaborative learning allows students to engage in meaningful discussions, share diverse perspectives, and work together to solve problems. It helps foster a sense of community in the classroom and prepares them for real-world scenarios where teamwork is essential.

In collaborative settings, young minds learn to negotiate roles, listen actively to others, and leverage the strengths of their peers. This encourages accountability and responsibility, as each member has a role in the group's success.

Example Session: Collaborative Science Project

Objective: Explore how pollution affects marine life and brainstorm solutions to reduce environmental impact.

Step 1: Attendees are divided into small groups and each group is assigned a different aspect of pollution (e.g., plastic waste, chemical runoff, oil spills).

Step 2: Within each group, students research their topic, identifying its causes, effects on marine ecosystems, and potential solutions.

Step 3: Groups then collaborate on creating a presentation or model that illustrates their findings and proposed solutions. For example, they might design an eco-friendly product, create a public awareness campaign, or develop a school-wide recycling program.

Step 4: Groups present their work to the class, followed by a peer feedback session to encourage cross-group collaboration and idea refinement.

> ➤ Through this process, youngsters not only learn about the environmental issue but also develop collaboration, communication, and leadership skills, as they contribute their unique strengths to the group's collective effort.

Aspect 10: **Modelling Creative Thinking**

This aspect involves demonstrating how to approach problems with curiosity, flexibility, and a willingness to experiment with new ideas. By actively showing students how you think through challenges, you set a standard for how they can approach their own learning creatively.

Real Example: "Design a New Classroom Tool"

Objective: Encourage the young generation to think creatively about everyday challenges and solutions.

Step 1: Teacher introduction (Modeling the Process). The educator begins the session by sharing a challenge: "We often have trouble keeping the classroom tidy by the end of the day. What if we could invent a tool that helps keep things organized more easily?"

The instructor then models creative thinking out loud: "Let me brainstorm. What kinds of tools could help? Maybe something that sorts pencils automatically, or a chair that doubles as a storage unit. What if there was a recycling bin that could talk and remind us when it's full?"

Step 2: Encourage learners to model different creative solutions. The teacher encourages students to brainstorm their own ideas in small groups. The focus is on letting pupils suggest "wild" or unusual ideas without worrying about them being practical at first. This encourages creative thinking without limitations.

Step 3: Reflect and iterate. Once ideas are shared, the teacher models reflection: "Let's take a closer look at one of my ideas - the talking recycling bin. Is it realistic? How could we make it work with the technology we have? Or, could we simplify it into a reminder system that lights up when full?"

Youngsters follow this model by refining their own ideas. They discuss what features of their creations might work and what challenges they may face. The instructor emphasizes that even imperfect ideas can lead to better solutions, modeling flexibility and adaptability.

Step 4: Prototyping or visual representation. Groups either sketch their tool or create a simple prototype with available materials (e.g., cardboard, paper). As they work, the teacher moves around, offering suggestions, and asking open-ended questions like, "What inspired this feature?" or "How else could you solve this problem?"

Step 5: Sharing and feedback. Each group presents their tool, explaining the creative process behind it. The mentor models constructive feedback, highlighting creative aspects and encouraging further thinking: "I love the way you've integrated a reminder system. What if it could also suggest recycling tips?"

➤ Through this session, the teacher not only demonstrates creative problem-solving but also encourages young minds to take risks and explore ideas without fear of failure. This approach shows them how creative thinking can lead to innovative solutions in any setting, including their everyday lives.

To sum up: **Embracing Creative Thinking in the Classroom**

As I mentioned before creative thinking is not just a skill but a mindset that can transform both teaching and learning. In today's ever-evolving world, it's vital that educators foster an environment where creativity thrives, enabling young individuals to think critically, solve complex problems, and adapt to new challenges with confidence.

Throughout this book, we've explored essential strategies that highlight the importance of integrating creative thinking into classroom practices. Let's reflect on these tactics and how they come together to create a dynamic, effective, and inspiring learning environment.

Classroom Discussions

Classroom discussions are a powerful tool for encouraging open-ended thinking. By prompting pupils to express their thoughts, opinions, and solutions, instructors nurture an atmosphere where every voice is valued. This open exchange of ideas helps students develop critical thinking skills and learn to respect diverse perspectives. This was the very first approach I started to use in my classes.

Providing a Safe Space for Ideas

A safe and supportive classroom is crucial for fostering creativity. That builds confidence in younger minds. When pupils feel comfortable sharing ideas without fear of judgment or failure, they're more likely to take intellectual risks. This kind of environment allows youngsters to explore their thoughts freely, making mistakes part of the learning process rather than something to avoid.

Group Brainstorming Sessions

Collaborative brainstorming taps into the collective creativity of a group, allowing students to build on each other's ideas. This aspect develops teamwork skills. By working together, young people learn to think in innovative ways, generating solutions they might not have come up with individually. These sessions also teach important skills like collaboration, communication, and the ability to compromise.

Mistake Celebration Sessions

Mistakes are often seen as setbacks, but they're actually vital opportunities for growth. When teachers celebrate mistakes, they teach students to view failure as a stepping stone to success. This approach encourages resilience and a growth mindset, where the young generation learns that experimentation and risk-taking are valuable components of the creative process.

Anonymous Idea Submission

Providing attendees with an anonymous platform to submit their ideas can unleash a torrent of creativity. When children don't fear being judged, they are more likely to contribute bold and innovative ideas. This method promotes inclusivity, ensuring that even the most introverted or shy individual can participate actively in the creative process. This aspect also prevents shyness and encourages confidence in expressing ideas.

Student-Led Projects

Giving class participants the responsibility to lead their own projects fosters a sense of ownership and accountability. Student-led projects encourage independent thinking, creativity, and leadership skills. By guiding their own learning experiences, creative minds discover their passions and learn to apply innovative solutions to real-world challenges.

By Oleg Borysiuk

Promoting Divergent Thinking

Encouraging young individuals to think divergently, or outside the box, is key to fostering creativity. Divergent thinking involves exploring multiple possible solutions to a problem, rather than settling for the first answer that comes to mind. This type of thinking enhances problem-solving skills and inspires innovation across various subjects.

Integrating Cross-Disciplinary Learning

Creativity often blossoms at the intersection of different fields of knowledge. Cross-disciplinary learning encourages pupils to make connections between subjects, leading to a deeper understanding of concepts. By integrating science, art, math, and language arts, students can approach problems from a broader, more innovative perspective.

Utilizing Creative Problem-Solving Tasks

Presenting learners with creative problem-solving tasks pushes them to think critically and apply their knowledge in new ways. These tasks encourage individuals to analyze problems, generate ideas, and implement solutions, helping them develop the creativity and adaptability they will need in future careers.

Allowing Time for Reflection

Reflection is an essential component of creative thinking, as it provides students with the opportunity to pause and evaluate their work thoughtfully. This process not only encourages them to consider their achievements and areas for improvement but also deepens their understanding of the creative process. By reflecting, individuals develop self-awareness, learning to recognize their strengths and address their weaknesses, which is crucial for personal growth.

A Creative Glossary of 50 Terms Related to Creativity, Innovation, and Imaginative Thinking:

Brainstorming – Generating ideas through spontaneous and free-flowing group discussions.

Mind Mapping – Visual organization of ideas, connecting concepts through branches.

Divergent Thinking – Exploring multiple possible solutions to a problem.

Convergent Thinking – Narrowing down options to find a single, best solution.

Innovation – The process of turning creative ideas into practical solutions.

Lateral Thinking – Solving problems through indirect, creative approaches.

Inspiration – The process of being mentally stimulated to create something.

Prototype – An early model of an idea or product used to test concepts.

Iteration – Repeated cycles of improving and refining ideas or projects.

Design Thinking – A human-centered approach to innovation and problem-solving.

Blue-sky Thinking – Creative thinking that is open to any possibility, unbounded by constraints.

Imagination – The ability to form new ideas, images, or concepts not present to the senses.

Empathy Mapping – Understanding the emotions, needs, and challenges of users or audiences.

Creative Flow – A state of full immersion and focus in a creative task.

Collaboration – Working with others to generate and improve ideas.

Innovation Hub – A space where creativity and innovation are actively encouraged.

Storyboarding – Visualizing a narrative or idea step-by-step, often used in creative projects.

Ideation – The creative process of generating, developing, and communicating new ideas.

Curiosity – The desire to learn, explore, and understand new concepts.

Serendipity – Finding valuable or pleasant things unexpectedly while exploring ideas.

Synthesis – Combining different ideas or elements to form a coherent whole.

Incubation – Letting ideas develop subconsciously after initial exploration.

Creativity Block – A mental barrier that prevents ideas from flowing freely.

Aesthetic – The principles guiding the artistic or visual aspects of a project.

Disruptive Innovation – Innovation that radically changes industries or markets.

Doodle – A spontaneous, casual drawing that can spark creative thoughts.

Conceptualization – The process of forming a concept or idea.

Empowerment – Encouraging others to think creatively and take ownership of ideas.

Perspective Shift – Looking at a problem from a new or different viewpoint.

Tinkering – Experimenting with ideas or tools in a playful and exploratory way.

Metaphor – Using figurative language to represent one idea in terms of another.

Juxtaposition – Placing two ideas, concepts, or objects side by side for contrast or comparison.

Outside the Box – Thinking creatively, beyond the range of conventional limits.

Role-playing – Using characters or scenarios to explore ideas from different perspectives.

Reverse Engineering – Taking something apart to understand its design and function.

Socratic Questioning – Asking open-ended, probing questions to challenge assumptions.

Playfulness – Engaging in fun or light-hearted activities to spark creativity.

Hybridization – Blending different ideas or elements to create something new.

Rapid Prototyping – Quickly building a model to test an idea or concept.

Sketching – Rough drawing or drafting as a preliminary idea.

Abstract Thinking – Thinking beyond the literal, using symbols, concepts, and ideas.

Analogy – Drawing comparisons between similar situations to solve problems.

Reframing – Changing the way a problem or situation is viewed to find new solutions.

Simplicity – Reducing an idea to its core components for clarity and effectiveness.

Risk-taking – Being willing to experiment with bold or unconventional ideas.

Constraints – Limitations that can actually foster creativity by forcing new approaches.

Cross-pollination – Taking ideas from one field and applying them to another.

Intuition – Using a sense of "gut feeling" to guide creative decisions.

Hackathon – An event where people collaborate intensively on creative solutions.

Mindfulness – Being fully present and aware can enhance creative focus.

This glossary includes key terms and concepts that help facilitate and drive creative thinking and innovation.

10 Effective Games to Boost Creativity in the Classroom

Upside-Down Drawing

Description:
This creative exercise encourages students to draw an image upside down, helping them focus on shapes and lines rather than the whole object, enhancing their observational skills and creative thinking.

Instruction:
Provide class members with a simple picture (like a cat or a house). Ask them to turn it upside down and attempt to draw it from this perspective without flipping it.

Example:
A pupil draws an upside-down dog, paying close attention to each line, without letting their preconceived idea of a "dog" influence their work.

Outcome:
Young learners gain a fresh perspective on visual elements, improve attention to detail, and break away from typical ways of thinking, fostering more open-mindedness and flexibility.

Shape Shifters

Description:
A game that challenges learners to think creatively by transforming one basic shape into something entirely new, encouraging imaginative thinking and adaptability.

Instruction:
Give pupils a simple shape, such as a circle or triangle. Ask them to turn that shape into something completely different by adding details or combining it with other elements.

Example:
A student starts with a circle and transforms it into a spaceship by adding wings, windows, and thrusters.

Outcome:
Youngsters develop creative flexibility, practice thinking beyond the obvious, and learn how to use simple elements to create complex ideas.

Perfect School

Description:
Young creators design their vision of the "perfect school," allowing them to exercise creativity while thinking critically about what an ideal learning environment should include.

Instruction:
Ask participants to imagine their perfect school and either draw it or write a description. Encourage them to include aspects such as classroom design, subjects taught, extracurriculars, and any innovative features.

Example:
A pupil designs a school with treehouse classrooms, flexible schedules, and interactive virtual reality lessons for subjects like history and science.

Outcome:
Students learn to think innovatively about education and how environments and teaching methods can impact learning. They also practice articulating their ideas in a structured way.

Two Truths and a Lie

Description:
A fun icebreaker where participants share two true statements and one false statement about themselves. The rest of the class guesses which statement is the lie, fostering creative thinking and engagement.

Instruction:
Each student writes down two facts about themselves and one made-up statement. They present all three to the class, and the class must guess which one is the lie.

Example:

A pupil says, "I've been to Japan, I have three pets, and I can play the guitar." The lie turns out to be that he has three pets, but he actually only has one.

Outcome:

This game helps youngsters develop communication skills, engage creatively, and encourage critical thinking as classmates try to figure out the lie. It also fosters class bonding.

Product Advertisement

Description:

Attendees create an advertisement for a fictional or real product, focusing on creativity and persuasive communication.

Instruction:

Ask students to invent a product or use an existing one, then develop a short advertisement. They can present it as a poster, video, or live performance, highlighting the product's features and why people should buy it.

Example:

A young creator invents "The Homework Machine" - a device that completes all homework while you sleep. They create a colorful poster and perform a commercial, showcasing how the machine saves time and ensures perfect grades.

Outcome:
This activity encourages creativity, persuasive communication, and critical thinking. Participants learn about advertising techniques and apply them while engaging in imaginative thinking.

Chain Story

Description:
Learners collaboratively build a story by each contributing a sentence or paragraph, resulting in a creative and often unexpected narrative.

Instruction:
Start with a single sentence to begin the story. Then, each student adds the next part of the story, one after another, without knowing the full direction the story will take until it's finished. The goal is to think on their feet and contribute to a cohesive but creative narrative.

Example:
The instructor starts with: "Once upon a time, a cat discovered it could fly." A pupil continues with, "The cat decided to fly to the moon, where it met a talking tree," and the story evolves from there as each member adds their imaginative twist.

Outcome:
The activity promotes creative collaboration, quick thinking, and story development. It helps participants

By Oleg Borysiuk

practice listening, building on others' ideas, and stretching their imaginations.

The Reverse Game

Description:
Students tackle a problem by brainstorming the worst possible solutions first, then flipping those ideas to find creative, effective solutions.

Instruction:
Present a specific problem or challenge to the class. Ask participants to think of the most absurd, ineffective ways to solve it. After gathering their "bad" ideas, challenge them to reverse those suggestions into viable solutions.

Example:
If the problem is "How can we encourage students to participate more in class?" a person might suggest, "We could make participation a punishment!" The class would then reverse this to propose, "Instead, we could reward pupils for their contributions."

Outcome:
This game fosters creative thinking by encouraging the young generation to step outside conventional problem-solving methods. It promotes humor, teamwork, and a deeper understanding of the challenges at hand, leading to innovative solutions.

Character Creation Relay

Description:

In this fast-paced activity, learners collaboratively create unique characters by passing around a sheet of paper and adding to the character's traits, background, and story in a relay fashion.

Instruction:

Divide the class into small teams. Each group receives a sheet of paper with a character's name at the top. Students have one minute to write a trait or background detail for the character, then pass the paper to the next person. This continues until the paper has gone around the group several times.

Example:

A group starts with the character named "Sam the Brave." The first pupil writes, "Sam is a knight who loves chocolate." The next adds, "He has a pet dragon named Sparky," followed by another student who writes, "Sam is afraid of heights." At the end of the round, the teams share their character profiles.

Outcome:

This activity enhances creativity and collaboration as young creators build upon each other's ideas. It encourages quick thinking, teamwork, and imaginative storytelling, resulting in diverse and entertaining characters.

Odd One Out

Description:
In this activity, class members analyze a group of items or concepts to identify the one that does not belong, fostering critical thinking and reasoning skills.

Instruction:
Present students with a set of four or five related items (e.g., fruits, animals, shapes). Ask them to discuss in pairs or small groups which item is the "odd one out" and explain their reasoning.

Example:
The teacher presents the items: apple, banana, carrot, and grape. Pupils discuss and determine that "carrot" is the odd one out because it is a vegetable, while the others are fruits. They might also discuss that it grows underground, unlike the others.

Outcome:
This activity sharpens analytical skills and encourages attendees to think critically about categories and relationships. It promotes discussion and justifies their choices, enhancing their communication skills.

Superpowers Debate

Description:
In this engaging activity, participants debate the merits

and drawbacks of various superpowers, enhancing their critical thinking, reasoning, and persuasive speaking skills.

Instruction:

Divide the class into small teams and assign each group one unique superpower (e.g., invisibility, flight, super strength, telepathy). Each group prepares arguments for why their assigned superpower is the best, considering potential benefits and consequences. After preparation, teams present their arguments in a structured debate format.

Example:

One group argues for invisibility, stating it allows for privacy and stealth, while another supports flight, emphasizing the freedom and efficiency of travel. Learners take turns presenting their points and countering opponents' arguments.

Outcome:

The debate encourages young individuals to think critically about different perspectives and articulate their thoughts clearly. It fosters collaboration, as pupils must work together to form cohesive arguments, and helps build confidence in public speaking.

> It's very important to make learning interactive, fun, and less structured. While providing students with valuable problem-solving and critical-thinking skills you boost their knowledge and intelligence overall.

 By Oleg Borysiuk

Your Role as an Educator

As an educator, you play a crucial role in shaping the creative minds of the future. By modeling creative thinking, providing opportunities for collaboration, and encouraging risk-taking, you're helping to unlock your students' potential. The strategies and activities outlined in this book are designed to empower you to create a vibrant, engaging, and supportive classroom environment where creativity can flourish.

As you move forward, remember that fostering creativity is not about following a rigid set of rules but about being flexible and open to new ideas. Every classroom is different, and what works for one group of individuals may not work for another. The key is to remain adaptable and continue exploring creative approaches that resonate with your audience. By embracing creativity in all its forms, you're not only enhancing your students' learning experiences but also helping them become innovative thinkers and problem-solvers.

In Conclusion

Creative thinking is the engine that drives innovation, and by integrating it into your teaching, you're setting your students up for success. These ten aspects of fostering creativity offer a comprehensive framework for transforming your classroom into a hub of creative exploration. As you implement these strategies, you'll witness a positive impact on your pupils' confidence, curiosity, and ability to think independently.

The future belongs to those who dare to think differently, and by encouraging creative thinking, you're empowering individuals to become the innovators and leaders of tomorrow.

I truly hope you found this book both engaging and useful. I put my heart into delivering the information as clearly and effectively as possible to help you foster creativity in your classroom. Your honest review on my Amazon product page would mean the world to me - it's the best way to support my work and help more educators like yourself discover these strategies. Your feedback will inspire me to keep improving and creating valuable content. Thank you for being a part of this journey!

By Oleg Borysiuk